NASCAR RACING

Bristol Motor Speedway

by A. R. Schaefer

Consultant:
Suzanne Wise, Librarian
Stock Car Racing Collection, Belk Library
Appalachian State University
Boone, North Carolina

Capstone *press*®
Mankato, Minnesota

Edge Books are published by Capstone Press,
151 Good Counsel Drive, P.O. Box 669, Mankato, Minnesota 56002.
www.capstonepress.com

Library of Congress Cataloging-in-Publication Data
Schaefer, A. R. (Adam Richard), 1976-
    Bristol Motor Speedway / by A.R. Schaefer.
    p. cm.—(Edge Books NASCAR racing)
    Includes bibliographical references and index.
    ISBN-13: 978-0-7368-4376-8 (hardcover)
    ISBN-10: 0-7368-4376-0 (hardcover)
1. Racetracks (Automobile racing)—Tennessee—Bristol—Juvenile literature. I. Title.
    II. Series.
GV1033.5.B757S35 2007
796.72'06875572—dc22   2005037072

Summary: Discusses the track design, history, and exciting races at Bristol Motor Speedway.

Editorial Credits
Tom Adamson, editor; Jason Knudson, set designer; Patrick D. Dentinger,
    book designer; Jo Miller, photo researcher

Photo Credits
AP Wide World Photos/Mark Humphrey, 6, 22
Corbis/New Sport/George Tiedemann, 19
Getty Images Inc./Jon Ferrey, cover; Rusty Jarrett, 11, 28; Donald Miralle, 12; David
    Taylor, 14; Robert Laberge, 16; Focus on Sport, 25; Jamie Squire, 27
The Sharp Image/Sam Sharpe, 5, 9, 13, 15, 21, 26, 29

Table of Contents

CHAPTER 1

Last Lap Spinout

Stock cars growled under the lights at Bristol Motor Speedway (BMS) on August 28, 1999. The Goody's 500 was a 500-lap night race. At least 140,000 people filled the stands.

NASCAR legend Dale Earnhardt Sr. started the race in 26th position. Only 65 laps later, he was in the top 10. On lap 299, officials waved the yellow flag for a caution. Most of the drivers took a pit stop. Earnhardt didn't. After the race restarted, he was in second place behind Terry Labonte, who also didn't stop.

Earnhardt and Labonte battled for the lead for the rest of the race. Labonte looked like the winner with 10 laps to go. Then, the leaders caught up to lapped cars. As Earnhardt and Labonte quickly got closer, the slower cars suddenly crashed. Labonte slowed to avoid the mess. Darrell Waltrip hit him from behind.

Dale Earnhardt and Terry Labonte battled at Bristol in 1999.

Learn about:

→ A close race

→ Earnhardt's bump move

→ Bristol basics

Dale Earnhardt celebrates one of his many Bristol victories.

Labonte took a pit stop to get four new tires during the caution, which gave the lead to Earnhardt. When Labonte returned in fifth position, he knew his tires would have better grip than Earnhardt's.

The green flag flew with five laps to go. Labonte raced by other drivers and pulled even with Earnhardt on the 498th lap. He passed Earnhardt as they drove under the white flag for one lap to go.

Earnhardt edged up to within inches of Labonte's car. Earnhardt then tapped Labonte's back bumper. Labonte spun out and crashed into the wall. Earnhardt raced to the checkered flag while the fans booed.

NASCAR officials looked at video replay to decide if Earnhardt broke the rules. They said that the move was legal. Earnhardt won the Goody's 500, his ninth win at Bristol.

"Typical Bristol. That's what keeps them packed in here."
—Sterling Marlin, after the 1999 race, 8-30-99, AP

Bristol Motor Speedway

Bristol Motor Speedway in Bristol, Tennessee, is the favorite track of many NASCAR fans. This short track is only about a half mile (.8 kilometer) long. Its turns have the steepest banking of any NASCAR track. The short track and high banking usually lead to exciting races.

Since it opened in 1961, BMS has hosted two NASCAR Cup Series races each year. One race is held during the spring, and the other takes place in late summer. At least 160,000 people usually attend races at Bristol. People call Bristol the "World's Fastest Half Mile."

"What can I say about Bristol? It's still a cantankerous, exciting, aggressive, anything-you-want-to-call-it race track."
—Dale Earnhardt Sr., 8-30-99, AP

Sitting in the stands at Bristol is a bit like being in a football stadium.

CHAPTER 2

Track Design

In 1960, Larry Carrier and Carl Moore saw a race at Charlotte Motor Speedway in North Carolina. They decided to build a new racetrack in Tennessee. Instead of building a 1.5-mile (2.4-kilometer) track like Charlotte, they built a half-mile (.8-kilometer) track.

Early Days

Bristol held its first NASCAR race on July 30, 1961. It was called the Volunteer 500. The stands held 18,000 people. Two drivers won that first race. Jack Smith started as the driver. Part way through the race, heat from the bottom of the car burned his right foot. Johnny Allen took over and finished the race for Smith. The two drivers shared $3,025 for winning the race.

Because Bristol is a short track, pit road can get crowded.

Learn about:

- → Bristol history
- → Banking
- → Short track action

Extreme banking helps drivers keep high speeds on sharp turns.

In 1969, the track was redesigned to make the banked turns higher. The banking went from 22 degrees to 36 degrees. The new track also became slightly longer. The half-mile track turned into a .533-mile (.9-kilometer) track.

"It's intense racing, one of those places where you can never take a break or you'll be in the wall."

—Dale Earnhardt Jr., 3-23-04, nascar.com

Popular Track

More seats have been added to BMS. At the beginning of 1996, BMS had seating for 71,000 people. Just seven years later, that number increased to more than 160,000 seats.

Races at BMS are popular because of the racing action. Most NASCAR races take place at large speedways. Bristol is different. BMS is banked so high and the track is so small that it almost looks like a football stadium. More than 40 cars on a short track at high speeds usually means many wrecks and exciting races.

Wrecks are common on a short track with high speeds.

The BMS track is shaped like an oval. It has two main straightaways. They are 650 feet (198 meters) long and banked at 16 degrees. The corners are banked at 36 degrees. The track is 40 feet (12 meters) wide. Bristol has a pit road on each straightaway. The track is not big enough for all the cars to pit on one straightaway.

Drivers gain speed on the straightaways.

The cars' brakes get so hot they glow.

Because of the tight corners, drivers do more braking than usual at Bristol. The cars' brakes get very hot and can wear down quickly. Teams put bigger brakes on the race cars than they would at other tracks. They also use cooling ducts. These hoses bring cool air to the brakes to keep them from overheating.

Drivers don't have to slow down much in the corners.

Centrifugal Force

In tight corners, drivers have to battle against centrifugal force. Centrifugal force causes speeding cars to slide to the outside and into the wall. Drivers usually have to slow down in the corners to avoid this skidding.

At Bristol, the high banking lets drivers go much faster around the corners. Steep banking has less centrifugal force. Cars speed down the straightaways at about 130 miles (209 kilometers) per hour. They slow down to no less than 100 miles (161 kilometers) per hour in the corners. The high banking keeps the races fast and exciting.

TRACK DIAGRAM
Bristol Motor Speedway

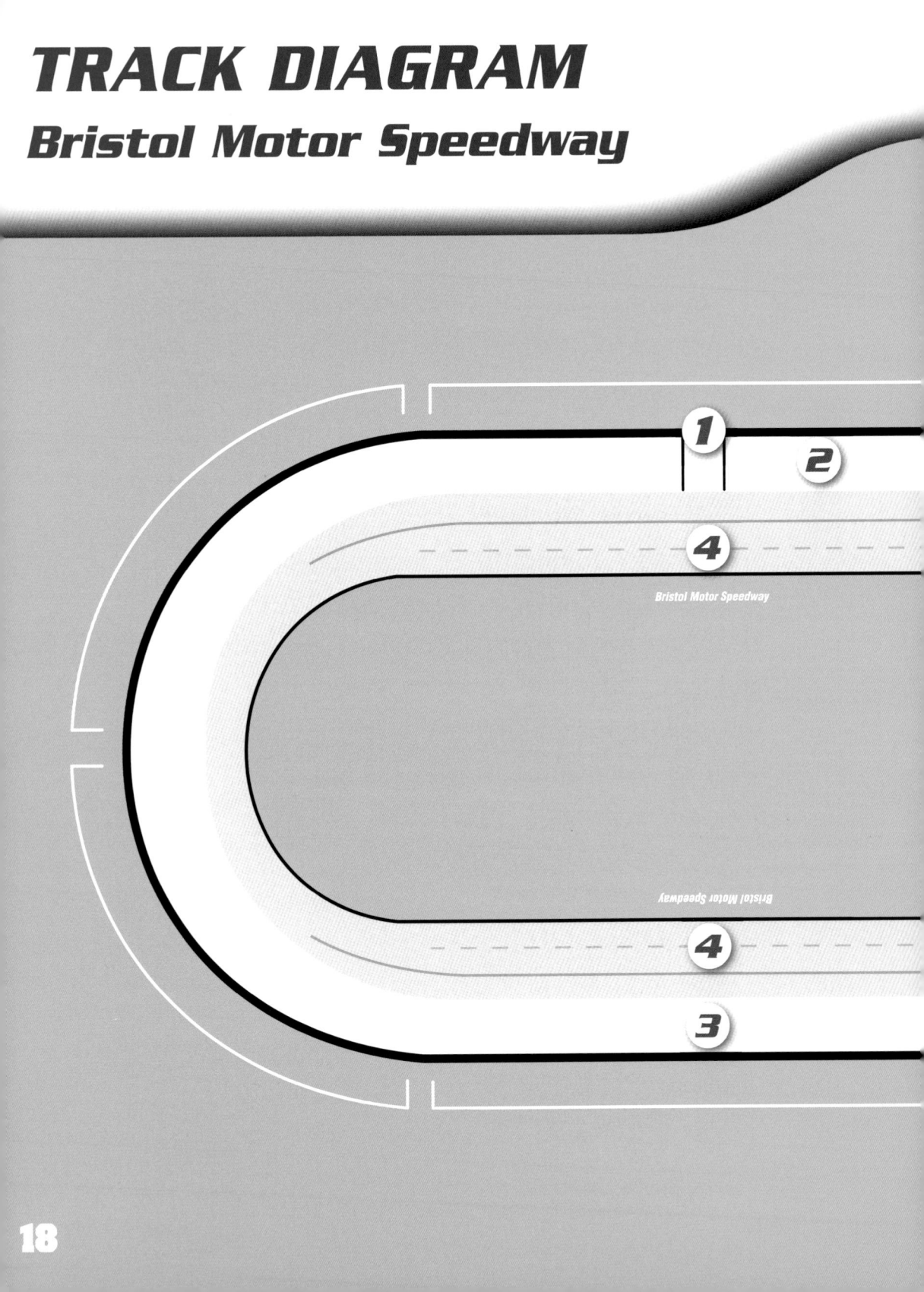

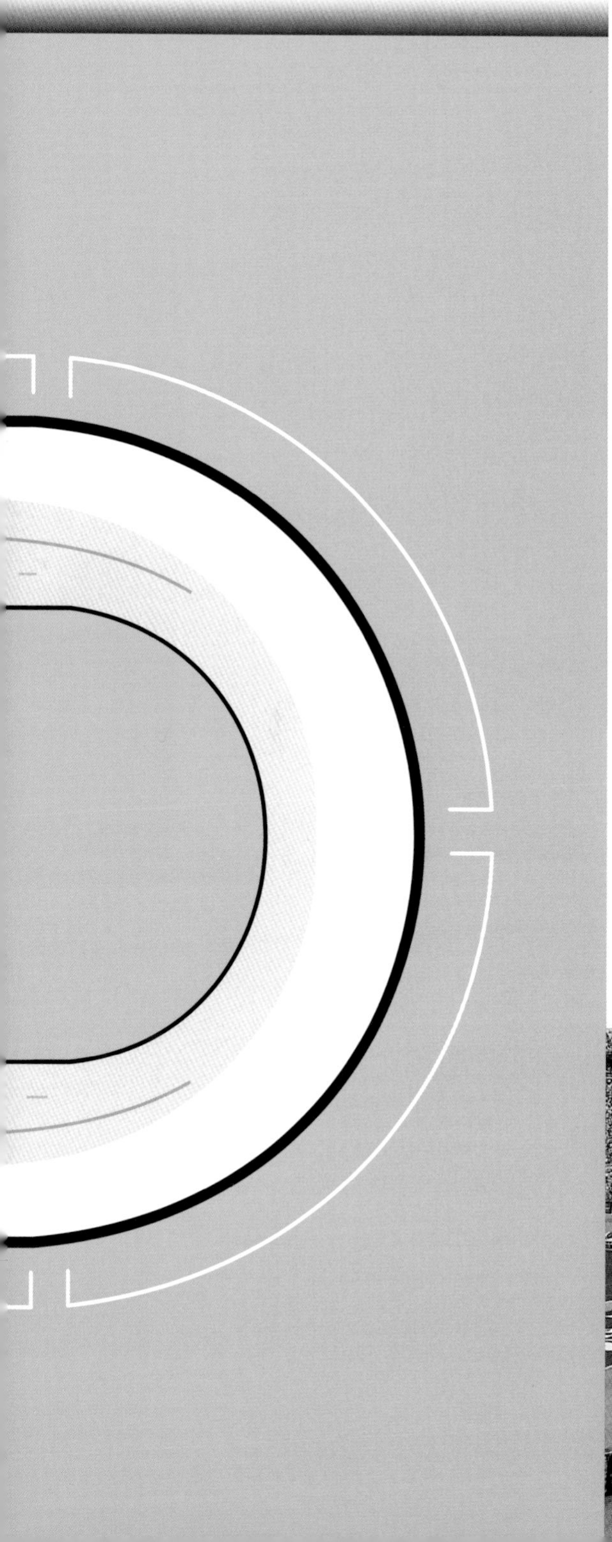

1. **Start-finish line**
2. **Frontstretch**
3. **Backstretch**
4. **Pit road**

CHAPTER 3

Famous Finishes

The short track, high banking, and fast speeds at Bristol combine for some of the best finishes in stock car racing. Some of the most memorable final laps have been at Bristol.

Close Calls

In the 1997 Food City 500, nine-time Bristol winner Rusty Wallace had a fast car. He was in the lead for 240 of the 500 laps. On the last lap, Wallace was leading and Jeff Gordon was right behind him. In the third turn, Gordon tapped Wallace from behind. Wallace lost control for only a second. It was enough for Gordon to sneak by just a few hundred feet from the checkered flag. Gordon won the race and left Wallace furious about the aggressive move.

Jeff Gordon and Rusty Wallace have had many duels at Bristol. Here, they race side-by-side in 2001.

Learn about:

→ Gordon's aggressive move

→ More Bristol bumping

→ A boring race

In 1995, Dale Earnhardt and Terry Labonte crashed on the final lap of the Goody's 500. Earnhardt was behind Labonte. Earnhardt tapped Labonte's car. Labonte's car went into a spin. But Earnhardt's bump didn't work. Labonte's car slid backward across the finish line just ahead of Earnhardt's.

Labonte won at Bristol in 1995, despite ending up with a destroyed race car.

Not Such a Close Call

Not every finish at Bristol is a nail-biter. One of the most boring races in NASCAR history took place there. In 1977, Cale Yarborough won the pole position. From his position in the front of the field, he led all but five laps. By the time he crossed the finish line for the victory, the closest car to him was seven laps behind.

"Rarely do the competitors leave Bristol happy, except for the guy who wins, and he probably has a few people mad at him."

—Jeff Gordon, September 2002, *Stock Car Racing*

CHAPTER 4

Bristol's Best

A few drivers have dominated Bristol's NASCAR races over the years. In the 56 Cup races at Bristol between 1973 and 2000, four drivers won 39 of them.

Darrell Waltrip

Darrell Waltrip holds the record for the most Cup wins at Bristol. He won 12 races at the track. His first win was in 1978. In 1981, Waltrip started an incredible streak. He won the race in March. He won again there in August. Then he won both races in 1982. Only Cale Yarborough had ever won four straight races at Bristol.

Waltrip kept going. He won both races in 1983 and the first one in 1984 before Terry Labonte beat him. Waltrip's seven straight wins at Bristol is still a record.

The Winston

GOODYEAR Winston Winston

DARRELL WALTRIP

Learn about:

→ **Waltrip's dominance**

→ **Bristol winners**

→ **A new Bristol threat**

Before retiring in 2005, Rusty Wallace won at Bristol nine times.

Nine Wins Each

Three other drivers have each won nine Cup races at Bristol. Cale Yarborough won half of the Bristol races between 1973 and 1980, including four straight in 1976 and 1977. He also won the pole position at Bristol nine times.

Rusty Wallace had long-term success at Bristol. He won his first race there in 1986. After that, he won eight more, including both races in 2000. He also won seven pole positions at Bristol.

Fan favorite Dale Earnhardt Sr. also won nine races at BMS. His first Cup win came at Bristol in 1979 when he was a rookie. Over the next 20 years, he won eight more times. His last win at Bristol was in 1999.

Dale Earnhardt intimidated other drivers at Bristol for many years.

Recent Bristol Stars

Jeff Gordon has won five races at Bristol through 2005. Gordon sometimes gets booed at Bristol. His aggressive moves and bumps have earned him several wins, but not many friends.

Jeff Gordon does a victory burnout at Bristol.

Kurt Busch has found that Bristol matches his driving style well.

Kurt Busch got his first Cup win at Bristol in 2002. In March 2004, Busch won his third straight race at Bristol. When he won that race, he was only 26 years old. He has the talent and driving style to threaten the records set at Bristol by NASCAR's legends.

"It's a place where everything happens so quick you have to adjust to it."
—Kurt Busch, 3-26-04, nascar.com

Glossary

aggressive (uh-GRESS-iv)—strong and forceful

banking (BANGK-ing)—the angle of the track; if a track has a high bank, the top of the track is much higher than the bottom of the track.

caution (KAW-shun)—a time during a race when drivers have to slow down and are not allowed to pass; a caution occurs after a crash or when the track crew has to clean up debris.

centrifugal force (sen-TRIF-yuh-guhl FORSS)—the physical force that causes a body rotating around a center to move away from the center

cooling ducts (KOOL-ing DUHKTS)—hoses that bring cool air to the race car's brakes to keep them from getting too hot

dominate (DOM-uh-nate)—to rule; in sports, a team or person dominates if they win much more than anyone else.

rookie (RUK-ee)—a first-year driver

straightaway (STRAYT-uh-way)—the longest, flattest part of a racetrack; a racetrack usually has a front straightaway and a back straightaway.

Read More

Cavin, Curt. *Terrific Tracks: The Coolest Places to Race.* The World of NASCAR. Maple Plain, Minn.: Tradition Books, 2004.

Peterson, Brian C. *Rusty Wallace: Short Track to Success.* The World of NASCAR. Maple Plain, Minn.: Tradition Books, 2004.

Schaefer, A. R. *Dale Earnhardt.* NASCAR Racing. Mankato, Minn.: Capstone Press, 2007.

Internet Sites

FactHound offers a safe, fun way to find Internet sites related to this book. All of the sites on FactHound have been researched by our staff.

Here's how:

1. Visit *www.facthound.com*

2. Choose your grade level.

3. Type in this book ID **0736843760** for age-appropriate sites. You may also browse subjects by clicking on letters, or by clicking on pictures and words.

4. Click on the **Fetch It** button.

FactHound will fetch the best sites for you!

Index